BOOK

OPERATION TIMOTHY

P.O. Box 8009
Chattanooga, TN 37414

Workbook chapters 7, 8, 9, 10 and 12 are adapted from *Design For Discipleship*, ©1973, 1978 by The Navigators, used by permission. All rights reserved, including translation.

Workbook chapter 11, Putting Your Testimony to Work, ©1980 by Christian Business Men's Committee of USA. All rights reserved, including translation.

Scripture quotations are from the *New International Version*, ©1978 by the New York International Bible Society, used by permission of Zondervan Bible Publishers.

Operation Timothy, ©1980, 1985 by Christian Business Men's Committee of USA. All rights reserved, including translation.

Operation Timothy Workbook 2 - ISBN 978-1-947457-26-3

Timothy, be strong in the grace that is in Christ Jesus. And the things you have heard me say in the presence of many witnesses entrust to reliable men who will also be qualified to teach others."

"My son,

Paul

OPERATION TIMOTHY

Table of Contents

CHAPTER SEVEN

HOW TO APPLY GOD'S WORD TO YOUR LIFE

A sword is to be used skillfully in battle as both an offensive and a defensive weapon. God has equipped you with such a weapon for your spiritual battle: "the sword of the Spirit, which is the word of God" (Ephesians 6:17). The Holy Spirit uses the word of God to accomplish the work of God.

> *"The great need of the hour among persons spiritually hungry is twofold: first, to know the Scriptures, apart from which no saving truth will be vouchsafed by our Lord; the second, to be enlightened by the Spirit, apart from whom the Scriptures will not be understood."*
>
> —A. W. TOZER*

GOD'S WORD— HIS COMMUNICATION TO YOU

The Bible is the most remarkable book ever written. The writing was done by about forty men of many occupations. They wrote over a period of approximately 1,500 years, and in three languages—Hebrew, Aramaic, and Greek. Yet the Bible has one great theme and central figure—Jesus Christ. All of this would be impossible unless the Bible had one supreme Author—and it did: the Holy Spirit of God.

1. What does 2 Timothy 3:16 say about the Scriptures? (Circle the letter of the correct answer.)

*From *The Root of the Righteous* (Harrisburg, Pennsylvania: Christian Publications, 1955), page 37.

a. Some of the Bible is inspired by God.
b. All of it is inspired by God.
c. Only the parts that speak to you in a personal way are inspired by God.

> *Inspired* comes from a Greek word meaning "God-breathed."

> *"The meaning, then, is not that God breathed into the writers, nor that he somehow breathed into the writings to give them their special character, but that what was written by men was breathed out by God. He spoke through them. They were his spokesmen."*
>
> —JOHN R. W. STOTT*

2. How was Scripture given? *2 Peter 1:20-21*

Who, then, helps you understand the Bible?
1 Corinthians 2:12-13

THE BIBLE AT A GLANCE (66 BOOKS)

OLD TESTAMENT (39 books)			"The New is in the Old concealed. The Old is in the New revealed."	NEW TESTAMENT (27 books)		
HISTORY 17 books	**POETRY** 5 books	**PROPHECY** 17 books		**HISTORY** 5 books	**TEACHING** 21 books	**PROPHECY** 1 book
Law	Job	**Major prophets**		**Gospels**	**Paul's letters**	Revelation
	Psalms				Romans	
Genesis	Proverbs	Isaiah		Matthew	1 Corinthians	
Exodus	Ecclesiastes	Jeremiah		Mark	2 Corinthians	
Leviticus	Song of	Lamentations		Luke	Galatians	
Numbers	Solomon	Ezekiel		John	Ephesians	
Deuteronomy		Daniel			Philippians	
				The early church	Colossians	
History and government		**Minor prophets**			1 Thessalonians	
				Acts	2 Thessalonians	
Joshua		Hosea			1 Timothy	
Judges		Joel			2 Timothy	
Ruth		Amos			Titus	
1 Samuel		Obadiah			Philemon	
2 Samuel		Jonah				
1 Kings		Micah			**General letters**	
2 Kings		Nahum			Hebrews	
1 Chronicles		Habakkuk			James	
2 Chronicles		Zephaniah			1 Peter	
Ezra		Haggai			2 Peter	
Nehemiah		Zechariah	About 400 years between testaments		1 John	
Esther		Malachi			2 John	
					3 John	
					Jude	

(The Old Testament looks forward to Christ's sacrifice on the cross. The New Testament is based on the work Christ finished on the cross.)

God used forty different men over a period of 1,500 years (about 1400 B.C. to A.D. 90) in writing the Bible.

*From *Understanding the Bible* (London: Scripture Union, 1972), page 183.

3. How do the following verses describe God's word?

Matthew 24:35 _____

John 17:17 _____

Hebrews 4:12 _____

4. Examine Psalm 19:7-11 carefully. Use the following chart to aid you in your investigation.

VERSE	WHAT THE BIBLE IS CALLED	ITS CHARACTERISTICS	WHAT IT WILL DO FOR ME
7	Law	perfect	refreshes spiritually
	Statutes	trustworthy	gives wisdom
8			
9			
10			
11			

In the chart above, place a check by the two or three thoughts which impressed you most about the Bible.

> "It is the very nature and being of God to delight in communicating himself. God has no selfishness. God keeps nothing to himself. God's nature is to be always giving."
> —ANDREW MURRAY*

HOW THE BIBLE HELPS YOU

5. Look up the following verses and summarize some of the ways the Bible is important to you as a Christian.

*From *Absolute Surrender* (Chicago: Moody Press, 1962), page 21.

Jeremiah 15:16 _____

John 5:39 _____

2 Peter 1:4 _____

1 John 2:1 _____

6. Analogy is a form which explains something by comparing it point by point with something similar. In the following verses, what is God's word compared with? What is the function of these objects?

	OBJECT	FUNCTION
Jeremiah 23:29		
Matthew 4:4		
James 1:23-25		

YOUR RESPONSIBILITY

7. "The Glories of God's Word" is a title given to Psalm 119. Nearly every verse of the psalm speaks of his word, and about applying it in daily living. Notice the psalmist's attitudes and actions concerning God's word. Beginning with verse 9, fill in the diagram below.

VERSE	ATTITUDE	ACTION
9		Keeping God's Word → pure life
10	Wholeheartedly sought God	Prayed —"Don't let me wander"
11		Hid Word in his heart
12		Asked God to teach him
13		
14		
15		
16		

8. According to John 8:31, what qualifies a man to be Christ's disciple?

_____

How would you explain these words to another person?

_____

_____

9. From the following verses fill in the remaining blanks.

	ACTION TO TAKE	WHY
Psalm 78:5-7		
Acts 17:11		
James 1:22		
Revelation 1:3		

10. Ezra is a good example of a man who felt a responsibility toward God's word. What was his approach to Scripture? *Ezra 7:10*

_____

_____

_____

_____

Note the order of Ezra's actions. He applied the Scriptures to his own life before he taught them to others.

SCRIPTURE   APPLIED   EZRA   APPLIED   OTHERS

11. Reflect carefully on Colossians 3:16.

a. What practical steps can you take to allow Christ's word to dwell in you richly? (Examples: take notes during sermons; write out memory verses.)

_____

_____

_____

_____

_____

b. Number them in the order of effectiveness for yourself.

c. During the next week, how can you put into practice the first two methods you numbered?

_____

_____

_____

_____

Romans 10:17 **Hear**
Revelation 1:3 **Read**
Acts 17:11 **Study**
Psalm 119:9-11 **Memorize**
Psalm 1:2-3 **Meditate**

These five methods of Scripture intake help you get a firm grasp on God's word.

THE IMPORTANCE OF MEDITATION

Meditation on the Scriptures is prayerful reflection with a view to understanding and application. The goal is to conform your life to God's will by prayerfully thinking how to relate God's word to yourself.

12. From Joshua 1:8, answer the following questions.

a. What should be the source of your meditation?

_____

b. Briefly state the relationship between meditation and application.

_____

_____

c. What are the results of meditation? _____

_____

13. Meditate on Psalm 1, and record your findings. Here are some questions to help you get started:

How is the Christian like a tree?

What are the differences between the godly and the ungodly man as to habits, stability, and future?

What new ideas from this psalm will help you in your relationship with God?

_____

_____

_____

_____

_____

_____

_____

_____

_____

_____

_____

_____

_____

_____

Remember These Points:

- God has communicated to man through his word— the Bible.
- Through the Scriptures you can get to know God better, understand his desires for your life, and discover new truths about living for him.
- God commands believers to let his word dwell richly in them. So it is important to give yourself wholeheartedly to allowing God's word to fill your life.
- God places emphasis on the act of meditating in his word, because effective meditation leads to personal application.

NOTES

_____

_____

_____

_____

_____

_____

_____

_____

_____

_____

_____

NEXT ASSIGNMENT

Workbook Chapter:

Memory verse:

Meeting Location:

Date: Time:

Additional Notes:

CHAPTER EIGHT

HOW TO KNOW GOD'S WILL

Sometimes it may seem to you that God's will is hidden in a buried treasure chest and you have only small portions of the map to find it. But is this true? Is God keeping his plans from you as some hidden secret? Or will he allow you to follow him, and lead you step by step?

Proverbs 3:5-6 can clear up misconceptions about knowing God's will. Meditate on it carefully: "Trust in the Lord with all your heart and lean not on your own understanding; in all your ways acknowledge him, and he will make your paths straight."

THE REVEALED WILL OF GOD

1. What should be one of your desires as a follower of Christ? *Ephesians 5:17*

_____

2. What does God promise you concerning his will for your life? *Psalm 32:8*

_____

_____

3. What does God reveal about his will for you in the following verses?

1 Thessalonians 4:3 _____

_____

1 Thessalonians 5:18 _____

_____

1 Peter 2:15 _____

_____

4. What was the psalmist's attitude toward God's will in Psalm 40:8?

_____

What actions help produce this attitude?_____

_____

5. Who is your source of strength to do God's will?

Philippians 2:13 _____

John 15:5 _____

> " The will of God is not like a magic package let down from heaven by a string . . . . The will of God is far more like a scroll that unrolls every day. . . . The will of God is something to be discerned and to be lived out every day of our lives. It is not something to be grasped as a package once for all. Our call, therefore, is basically not to follow a plan or a blueprint, or to go to a place or take up a work, but rather to follow the Lord Jesus Christ. "
>
> —PAUL LITTLE*

We often face decisions on issues which the Scriptures do not provide specific instructions for. In these cases, a Christian should apply the *principles* of decision-making which are contained in Scripture.

PRINCIPLES OF DECISION-MAKING

Objectives from Scripture
God has given particular commandments which can help you make decisions concerning your activities. If a particular course of action is inconsistent with the Bible, then you know it is not his will for you.

*From *Affirming the Will of God* (Downers Grove, Illinois: InterVarsity Press, 1971), page 8.

12

6. Using the following verses, state in your own words some of God's objectives for you. God wants you to . . .

Matthew 6:33 _____

_____

Matthew 22:37-39 _____

_____

Matthew 28:18-20 _____

_____

1 Peter 1:15 _____

_____

2 Peter 3:18 _____

_____

Ask yourself some questions based on these and similar verses to determine your course of action:
a. Am I putting God's desire ahead of my own?
b. Will it help me to love God and others more?
c. How does this action relate to my personal involvement in fulfilling Christ's Great Commission?
d. Will this help me lead a more holy life?
e. Will this course of action increase my personal knowledge of Christ?

Honestly answering these questions will help you make a decision in accordance with God's word.

7. Using the following verses, develop questions that will help you discern God's will.

1 Corinthians 6:12 _____

_____

1 Corinthians 6:19-20 _____

_____

1 Corinthians 8:9 _____

_____

1 Corinthians 10:31 _____

_____

Obedience to God

If you refuse to obey God in what he has already shown you, why should God give you further direction? Obedience to the known will of God is important in receiving further guidance.

8. How do you gain an understanding of God's will?

Psalm 37:31 _____

Psalm 119:105,130 _____

9. What other action can you take to learn God's will?

Psalm 143:8 _____

James 1:5 _____

10. Psalm 25:4-5 is a prayer of David concerning God's direction for his life. Write this prayer in your own words, and use it now as a prayer of your own heart.

_____

_____

_____

_____

11. What conditions are given in Romans 12:1-2 for finding God's will?

_____

_____

_____

12. Whose guidance have you been promised as you seek direction from God? *John 16:13*

_____

13. Read Psalm 27:14 and Isaiah 30:18. How does "waiting on the Lord" relate to knowing God's will? How do you do it?

_____

_____

_____

_____

_____

Satan rushes men—God guides them.

Openness to God's Leading

Many difficulties in determining the Lord's will are overcome when you are truly ready to do whatever his will may be.

14. You may not always know all of the possible alternatives in determining what to do. What is a means by which you can gather additional information? *Proverbs 15:22*

_____

_____

Counsel should be obtained from mature Christians who themselves are committed to the will of God and who know you well. It helps to talk with others who have previously made decisions in matters you are presently experiencing.

15. Explain the principle Jesus used in answering those who were questioning him. *John 7:17*

_____

_____

_____

How does this apply to knowing God's will?_____

_____

_____

16. When you know what God wants you to do, how should you do it? *Ephesians 6:6*

_____

_____

17. What are other factors that can help you discern God's leading? Match the following verses with the appropriate phrase.

____ Careful and wise   a. *Colossians 3:15*
     thinking   b. *Romans 13:1*

____ Inner spiritual peace   c. *Ephesians 5:15-17*

____ Legal obligations

18. Examine the following examples from the Bible and ask yourself these questions: What decision was made? What was the major issue in this decision?

PERSON	DECISION
Gideon *Judges 6:25-28*	
Moses *Hebrews 11:25-26*	
Demas *2 Timothy 4:10*	

19. The following chart may be helpful in determining God's will for a particular decision you now face.

Decision I am facing: _____

SCRIPTURAL OBJECTIVES	YES	NO	NEUTRAL
Am I putting God's desire ahead of my own?			
Will it help me love God and others more?			
Will it help me to fulfill the Great Commission?			
Will it help me lead a more holy life?			
Will it help me further my Christian training?			

Other questions: _____

OBEDIENCE TO GOD
Are there other areas in which I need to obey God before determining this decision?

_____

_____

What have I seen recently in the Scriptures that relates to this decision?

_____

_____

Have I prayed about this decision?

_____

OPENNESS TO GOD'S LEADING
What are the various options I have in making this decision?

OPTIONS	ADVANTAGES	DISADVANTAGES

Am I truly willing to do whatever God wants me to?
What counsel have I received from others?

_____

_____

_____

With what decision do I feel inner spiritual peace?

_____

_____

_____

What circumstances relate to this decision?

_____

_____

_____

NOTES

_____

_____

_____

_____

_____

_____

_____

_____

_____

_____

_____

_____

_____

_____

_____

NEXT ASSIGNMENT

Workbook Chapter:

Memory verse:

Meeting Location:

Date: Time:

Additional Notes:

_____

HOW TO GIVE YOUR TIME, TALENT, AND TREASURE

Jesus Christ is Savior *and* Lord.

William Barclay has written, "Of all the titles of Jesus the title Lord became by far the most commonly used, widespread, and theologically important. It would hardly be going too far to say that the word Lord became a synonym for the name of Jesus."*

**THE LORD
JESUS CHRIST**

1. Titles reveal important information about the person to whom they refer. What are Jesus Christ's titles in the following verses?

John 13:13 _____

Acts 2:36 _____

Revelation 19:16 _____

Summarize what these titles reveal about Jesus Christ.

_____

2. Jesus Christ is Lord of (connect the following answers with the corresponding references):

Creation   Colossians 1:16-17

The living and the dead   Colossians 1:18

All Christians—the church   Romans 14:9

*From *Jesus as They Saw Him* (New York: Harper and Row, 1962), page 408.

Christ should have the same place in our hearts that he holds in the universe.

3. Write your own definition of the word *lord* as you feel it applies to Jesus Christ. (A dictionary may aid you here.)

_____

_____

_____

_____

4. Examine Philippians 2:9-11.

a. How has God exalted Jesus Christ?_____

_____

_____

b. How will every person exalt him?_____

_____

5. How do the angels acknowledge Christ's lordship in Revelation 5:11-12?

_____

_____

_____

6. Read 1 Corinthians 6:19-20.

a. How did you become God's possession?_____

_____

b. Therefore, what should you do?_____

_____

_____

Jesus Christ, Lord of lords, has always existed and always will. Not all people presently acknowledge him as their Lord, but that does not alter the fact of his lordship. All will someday acknowledge Christ as Lord, but the privilege of acknowledging and obeying his lordship is possible now. Allow Christ to be the Lord of your life—by *decision* followed by *daily practice.*

7. What place should Christ hold in a believer's life?
Colossians 1:18

_____

> *Christ is present in all Christians;*
> *Christ is prominent in some Christians;*
> *But in only a few Christians is Christ*
> *preeminent.*

8. What are we commanded to do in Romans 12:1?

_____

_____

Why should you do this?_____

_____

_____

_____

9. Check any of the sentences below which apply to you.

a. I generally think or feel that. . .

___Jesus doesn't really understand my problems.

___He may want me to do something I can't.

___He may want me to enter a career which I could
not enjoy.

___He will prevent me from getting married.

___He will take away my enjoyment of possessions,
hobbies, or friends.

___He can help me in the "big" things, but he
doesn't care about the little things.

b. Are there any other fears which have prevented you from giving Christ access to every area of your life?

_____

_____

c. How does the statement in Jeremiah 29:11 dispel these fears?

_____

_____

> "*A clear and definite activity of the will is involved in recognizing his lordship, since he is to be Lord of all. By her 'I will' the bride at the marriage altar, ideally, forever enthrones her groom in her affections. In subsequent years she lives out in detail all that was implied in that momentary act of the will. A similar enthronement of Christ can result from a similar act of the will, for the same decision as enthrones Christ automatically dethrones self.*"

—J. OSWALD SANDERS*

10. Consider the following questions and check the appropriate box:

	ME	JESUS
Who knows perfectly what is best for my life?	☐	☐
Who is most able to do what is best for my life?	☐	☐
Who desires at all times what is truly best for my life?	☐	☐

Why? _____

_____

_____

_____

11. Prayerfully meditate on the lordship of Christ. Have you decided to acknowledge Jesus' lordship in your life?

YES___   NO___

Explain your answer.

_____

_____

*From *The Pursuit of the Holy* (Grand Rapids, Michigan: Zondervan, 1972), page 65.

12. Good intentions don't guarantee good results. A good start does not ensure a strong finish—decision is only the beginning. Once you have decided to acknowledge the lordship of Christ in your life, you will prove that he *is* Lord by submitting to him hour by hour and obeying him in the daily affairs of life. Some of these areas are represented in the following illustration.

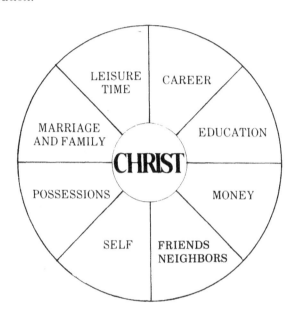

Take a few moments to evaluate your practice of the lordship of Jesus Christ in these areas. A good way to determine if Christ is in control is to ask, "Am I willing to do whatever Christ desires in this area?" or "Will I be able to thank God for whatever may happen in this area?"

a. Are there any areas in the illustration which you are not allowing Christ to control?

_____

_____

b. Are there other areas which you are not allowing Christ to control?

_____

_____

_____

c. What can you do in these areas to acknowledge Christ's lordship?

_____

_____

_____

_____

_____

We should not be concerned about what we would do for the Lord if we only had more money, time, or education. Instead, we must decide what we will do with the things we have now. And what really matters is not who or what we are, but whether Christ controls us.

13. Whenever you assume control of your life, you will soon become unhappy and anxious. What does the Bible say you can do? *1 Peter 5:6-7*

_____

_____

Based on this verse, draw this man's solution in the box provided.

14. What can happen if cares and worries are not committed to Christ? *Mark 4:18-19*

_____

_____

_____

_____

How do you think this takes place? _____

_____

_____

15. In Luke 9:23, what three things is the person who decides to follow Christ called to do? (Write them in your own words.)

_____

_____

_____

_____

16. Read Colossians 3:23-24. Underline the best answer below and explain why it is better than the other two:

Paul said a Christian should:

    Serve Christ more sincerely than he serves people.

    Not try to mix his religion and his everyday life.

    Do ordinary tasks wholeheartedly because he is really serving Christ.

_____

_____

_____

_____

17. According to Luke 6:46, what is a good way to evaluate if Christ is truly Lord of your life?

_____

_____

_____

18. Read Luke 18:28-30.

a. What had the apostles done? _____

_____

b. How did Jesus respond? _____

_____

19. What does the lordship of Christ mean to you personally?

_____

_____

_____

_____

_____

_____

_____

_____

Remember These Points:

- Jesus Christ is declared to be Lord in the Scriptures. He is worthy to be Lord because of who he is and what he has done.
- Because Jesus Christ is Lord, the Christian's responsibility is to acknowledge his authority every day in all areas of his life.
- Various areas of a believer's life may not be subject to the control of Christ. The Christian should submit these areas to Christ and continue to recognize that Christ's control of his life is for his own welfare and joy.

NOTES

_____
_____
_____
_____
_____
_____
_____
_____
_____
_____
_____
_____
_____
_____
_____
_____
_____
_____

NEXT ASSIGNMENT

Workbook Chapter:

Memory verse:

Meeting Location:

Date: Time:

Additional Notes:

CHAPTER TEN

HOW TO WITNESS FOR CHRIST

"It is the Holy Spirit, not we, who converts an individual. We, the privileged ambassadors of Jesus Christ, can communicate a verbal message; we can demonstrate through our personality and life what the grace of Jesus Christ can accomplish . . . . But let us never naively think that we have converted a soul and brought him to Jesus Christ . . . . No one calls Jesus Lord except by the Holy Spirit."

—PAUL LITTLE*

THE CHALLENGE

1. In Mark 5:18-19, notice Jesus' words to a man he had healed.

a. Where did he send him?

_____

b. What did he tell him to do?

_____

_____

c. Why do you suppose Jesus gave these particular instructions?

_____

*From *How to Give Away Your Faith* (Chicago: Inter-Varsity Press, 1966), page 53.

2. When you think about speaking of Christ, how do you react? (Either check a given sentence or write one of your own.)

___ I find it difficult to speak of such a personal matter.

___ I do not speak unless someone asks me.

___ I find it easy to talk to friends about Christ, but not people I don't know.

___ I find it easy to talk to strangers about Christ, but not close friends.

___ I often find myself talking to people about Christ, and I enjoy it very much.

_____

How do you think Peter would have answered this question? *Acts 4:20*

_____

_____

3. Sometimes you may feel as though you "need to know all the answers" before you can be an effective witness for Christ. What would you share with others? *1 John 1:3*

_____

_____

And for what purpose?

_____

_____

_____

How would you summarize the most important things you have seen and heard about Christ?

_____

_____

_____

_____

_____

4. Contrast the difference in the lives of the people in this chart:

	HOW DID THEY ACT?	WHY DID THEY ACT THIS WAY?
The Authorities (John 12:42-43)		
Paul (Romans 1:15-16)		

5. Carefully examine 2 Corinthians 5:9-14. In this section several motivations and reasons for witnessing for Christ are mentioned. List those you discover.

Verse 9 _____

Verse 10 _____

Verse 11 _____

Verse 14 _____

> *Witnessing is taking a good look at the Lord Jesus and then telling others what you've seen.*

HOW DO YOU BECOME AN EFFECTIVE WITNESS?

Witnessing is not merely an activity—it is a way of life. Christians don't *do* witnessing; they *are* witnesses—good or bad. Concentrate on improving your witness for Jesus Christ.

31

Witness by Love

6. Consider the qualities of love mentioned in
1 Corinthians 13:4-7. Which three do you feel would help you
most to become a more effective witness for Christ?

_____

_____

_____

7. Read John 13:34-35. Imagine yourself as one of the apostles,
and Jesus has just finished making this statement. What im-
mediately comes to your mind?

_____

_____

Why do you think Jesus gave this command?

_____

_____

Some people never read the Bible and seldom attend church.
If you want them to know what Christ can do for them, let them
see what Christ has done for you.

Witness by Life

8. What can be the results of your good works? _Matthew 5:16_

_____

9. Read 2 Corinthians 3:1-3. What was said to be true of
the Corinthians?

_____

_____

Do you think people notice your life and consider it a witness for
Jesus? Why or why not?

_____

_____

_____

_____

_____

"You are writing a gospel, a chapter each day,
by the deeds that you do and the words that you say.
Men read what you write—distorted or true;
What is the gospel according to you?"

Witness by Word

10. What challenge and instruction with regard to witnessing do you see in 1 Peter 3:15?

11. Some important facts about witnessing for Christ are given in 1 Corinthians 2:4-5. Paraphrase these verses.

12. The blind man whom Jesus healed had little or no theological training, but he was able to relate simply and effectively the facts of his experience. What did he say? *John 9:25*

33

Can you make a statement similar to that of the healed blind man? How would you say it in your own words?

_____

_____

_____

_____

> *"I cannot, by being good, tell men of Jesus' atoning death and resurrection, nor of my faith in his divinity. The emphasis is too much on me, and too little on him."*
>
> —SAMUEL SHOEMAKER*

PRESENTING CHRIST

13. Why is it important to present Jesus Christ to men who are lost?

John 14:6 _____

_____

Acts 4:12 _____

_____

14. Read John 3:16-18

a. What four points summarize the gospel? *Verse 16*

_____

_____

_____

_____

b. Why did God send Jesus into the world? *Verse 17*

_____

*From *Extraordinary Living for Ordinary Men* (Grand Rapids, Michigan: Zondervan Books, 1965), page 117.

c. What are two types of people? *Verse 18*

_____

_____

d. What one thing is necessary to escape condemnation?

_____

Be ready to speak of Christ in any situation: Know the essentials of the gospel. Plan and practice how to explain about Jesus Christ in a clear and interesting way. Then pray and take advantage of your opportunities.

NOTES

_____

_____

_____

_____

_____

_____

_____

_____

_____

_____

NEXT ASSIGNMENT

Workbook Chapter:

Memory verse:

Meeting Location:

Date: Time:

Additional Notes:

_____

36

CHAPTER ELEVEN

HOW TO PUT YOUR TESTIMONY TO WORK

BE PREPARED

1. In 1 Peter 3:15, Peter exhorts us to be prepared.

a. When should we be prepared? _____

b. What are we to be prepared to do? _____

c. What is meant by the phrase, *"the hope that you have?"*

_____

_____

**MAKE THE MOST OF
EVERY OPPORTUNITY**

In concluding his letter to the Colossians, Paul gives us some valuable insights into how we should witness. Carefully read Colossians 4:2-6 and answer the following questions.

2. In verse 2, Paul is communicating that the first step in any witnessing activity is an ongoing activity. What is that activity?

_____

3. In verses 3 and 4, three specific prayer requests concerning Paul's witness are made. What are they?

A. _____

B. _____

C. _____

4. What is being taught by Paul asking God to *"open a door for his message?"*

_____

Who's responsibility is it to open the door? _____

Who's responsibility is it to proclaim the message? _____

5. According to verse 5, how are we to act toward outsiders?

_____

Who are these outsiders? _____

What are we instructed to do with witnessing opportunities?

_____

6. Are we to converse (witness) with each person the same way? verse 6

_____

What will determine how we respond to each person?

_____

PAUL'S STORY

If we are to be *prepared,* what shall we do? How do we prepare? What do we say and how do we say it? How can we *make the most of every opportunity?*

In Acts 26, we find one of the most dramatic moments in the young New Testament church. Paul, arrested several years ago in Jerusalem is on his way to Rome to make his appeal to Caesar. In route he has an opportunity to share his testimony before Festus, Governor of Caesarea, and King Agrippa, the Roman representative in that part of Galilee. As you study this passage you will discover a number of key principles you can use in preparing your own testimony that you might *be prepared to make the most of every opportunity.*

7. In Acts 26:2-3, how is Paul's opportunity to make his defense to Agrippa described?

_____

How did he describe King Agrippa? _____

What did he ask the king to do in verse 3? _____

8. Why is the information in verses 4 and 5 shared? Would this be received negatively or positively by Paul's Jewish audience?

_____

_____

9. In verses 9 and 11, Paul continues to explain his background, his life before he became a Christian. What is the difference between this and what he said in verses 4 and 5?

_____

_____

10. According to verses 12-15, what happened to Paul to turn him away from the direction he was travelling to the new path of following Christ?

_____

_____

_____

11. In verse 16, why did Christ appear to Paul? _____

_____

How does this relate to 1 John 1:3? What are we to proclaim?

_____

12. What was Paul's response to Christ's command? *verse 19*

_____

13. In verse 23, Paul capsulates the gospel message. Contrast this to his message in 1 Corinthians 15:3-5. If you had to distill the gospel into three short points using these two passages of Scripture, what would they be?

A. _____

B. _____

C. _____

14. How is this message described in verse 25?

_____

15. What is the appeal in Paul's closing remark in verse 29?

_____

_____

16. What is meant when Paul says, *"I pray God that . . . you . . . may become what I am."*?

_____

PUTTING YOUR STORY TO WORK

"I wish I could turn this conversation around and tell him about Christ."

"If there were only more time, I could tell him what Christ means to me."

"I wish I could remember those verses about how someone can receive Christ."

"If Paul were here, he could really explain how to become a Christian."

How often have these thoughts and others like them crossed your mind as opportunities to share Christ presented themselves? You can turn day-to-day situations into exciting opportunities to share your faith by preparing ahead of time. Peter admonished us in I Peter 3:15 to be ready.

"But in your hearts set apart Christ as Lord. Always be prepared to give an answer to everyone who asks you to give the reason for the hope that you have."

There are three approach questions with real psychological force that follow in succession. They help determine a person's spiritual condition:
- Are you interested in spiritual things?
- Have you ever thought of becoming a Christian?
- Suppose someone were to ask you, *"What is a Christian?"* What would you say?

40

any subject can be presented more effectively by careful organization. A carefully prepared testimony, given in the power of the Holy Spirit, can be of immediate and effective use in nearly every witnessing situation. It should be our desire to present Christ in such a clear and attractive, yet simple, way that those who hear will not only want to know Him, but they will want to know Him in a personal way.

A carefully worded four-minute testimony will communicate far more effectively than a prolonged presentation that includes a lot of extraneous material. The key is to minimize details that detract from, rather than emphasize, the point of personal commitment to Christ and what this can mean in a person's life. What are the essentials for effectively presenting the gospel? Fortunately God has left us a model to follow. In Acts 26, we find Paul before King Agrippa giving his testimony. Read this passage carefully, using the outline below.

1. GRACIOUS INTRODUCTION -- 26:2, 3 -- "... I consider myself fortunate to stand before you today as I make my defense ..."

Notice that Paul referred to Agrippa's knowledge of Jewish customs. Find a point of common interest or identification. You might say to a friend, "Jim, I deeply value your friendship, and I'm ashamed that I've never told you how I met my best friend, Jesus Christ." Or, "You and I have a lot in common, Pete. When I was in school, I had everything a fellow could want, but underneath there was a lot of dissatisfaction." If the person has children, something along the following lines might be appropriate. "Bringing up children in this modern world is nearly impossible. Apart from one factor, I'd be utterly lost as to what to do." You should have several possible introductions you could use in a variety of situations.

2. GOOD PART OF PAST LIFE -- 26:4, 5 -- "... I lived as a Pharisee ..."

If you just say what a sinner you were, people won't identify themselves with you. Paul told how he was looked up to for his religious practices. If relevant, mention briefly your good points from a worldly sense, like morality, church attendance, ideas about God, generosity, as you lead to the third point.

41

3. BAD PART OF PAST LIFE -- *26:9-11* -- *". . . I, too, was convinced that I ought to do all that was possible to oppose the name of Jesus . . ,"*

"Even though people thought that I was so good, I knew what went on inside." Mention some specific things such as hateful thoughts, covetousness, emptiness of heart, or pride. Perhaps you feared that you would not go to heaven. Many will identify with you in this -- they're not sure they're going to heaven either.

4. CIRCUMSTANCES OF CONVERSION -- *26:12-15* -- *"Who are you, Lord?"*

Don't feel your own story is colorless compared to Paul's. Your conversion is as much a miracle as his. Your testimony doesn't have to be exciting, just interesting and "real" to your audience. Use details which show the personal transaction with God, and avoid confusing statements like "I went forward at church," lest your listener thinks going forward is the answer. Instead use, "When the minister asked if I had received Christ personally, I knew I had not and that this was the time I must trust Him." If you do not know the exact time you were saved, you could say: "The time came when I realized what I was doing was not enough, but that Jesus' death on the cross provided my salvation." We know the sun rises at an exact moment, but we may not have seen it right then. Yet we know it is there because we see it in the sky.

5. RESULTS OF CONVERSION -- *26: 16-22* -- *"I was not disobedient to the vision from heaven."*

Mention the most striking change in your life, as Paul did-- whether in desires, actions, hunger for God's Word, peace, or satisfaction. Show the effects of your being born-again. Be realistic. Don't imply that Christ eliminates all the problems of life, but rather that He enables you to live them out with peace and confidence.

6. GOSPEL MESSAGE -- *26:23* -- *"that the Christ would suffer and, as the first to rise from the dead . . ."*

Christ's story, His death for our sins and His resurrection, must be interwoven into your story. Without His involvement you would not have a story worth telling. Emphasize that the difference in your life was accepting Jesus Christ as Lord and Savior.

The order of Paul's story reflects the situation he was in and the people he was speaking to. Your message must have this type of flexibility. For example, you may find it beneficial to include the gospel explanation in point 4, making it part of the explanation of how you came to Christ. This portion of your testimony should include verses of scripture.

7. PERSONAL APPEAL -- *26:27-29* -- *"That . . . you may become what I am . . ."*

Using the listener's name, ask a question relating to him. "Bob, have you ever thought of Christ in this personal way?" "If you died today, would you go to heaven?" Or, "Does what I have said bring any question to your mind?"

HELPFUL HINTS FOR PREPARING YOUR TESTIMONY

1. Speak to God first, and ask Him to speak through you. Ask Him to give you wisdom and guidance as you write. (James 1:5, 6)

2. Follow a three-point outline:
    a. Life before knowing Christ.
    b. How you came to Christ (be specific).
    c. Life after you received Christ (changes He has made, what He means to you now).

3. Begin with an interesting, attention-getting sentence and close with a good conclusion. Include relevant, thought-provoking, personal experiences.

4. Write in such a way that others will identify with your past and present experiences.

5. Give enough detail to arouse interest.

6. Use some Scripture verses.

7. Avoid --

    a. using statements which reflect negatively on people or organizations.

    b. mentioning denominations.

    c. preaching at people. This is a testimony, not a preachamony.

    d. using stereotypes or overworked terms.

e. using words that are meaningless to non-Christians, e.g. "salvation," "saved," "Born again," "sanctified," etc. If this type of word must be used, it should be clearly explained.

8. Prepare your testimony so that you can share it in a group situation as well as with an individual.

9. Build your testimony around a theme—something characteristic of your life that is of general interest to non-Christians. Examples: personal success (your past vs. present perspective), life goals, etc.

10. Keep in mind that your testimony should give enough details so that someone else would know how to trust Christ after hearing how you did it.

It is important that Christ be lifted up as the only way to eternal life (John 14:6). Make sure this point is clearly made in your testimony.

Now you're ready to prepare your story. Use the three-point outline on the next page to quickly list the major points as they come to mind. When you write it out in more detail, keep it between 700 and 1000 words (if typewritten, about four double-spaced pages.) This will allow you to stay within three to five minutes when you give it verbally. Many men have found it helpful to take a first-pass at their testimony verbally and have a friend identify and jot down the major points on the outline.

As you begin, ask God to give you the right words and approach. Trust Him to do it. This is as much His story as it is yours.

I. LIFE BEFORE I TRUSTED CHRIST

_____

_____

_____

_____

_____

_____

II. HOW I CAME TO CHRIST (Be specific — this area needs the most detail)

_____

_____

_____

_____

_____

_____

_____

_____

_____

_____

_____

III. LIFE AFTER I TRUSTED CHRIST (Changes He has made, what He means to me now)

_____

_____

_____

_____

_____

HELPFUL HINTS FOR SHARING YOUR TESTIMONY

1. Be prepared to share your testimony and alert to opportunities that cross your path. As noted before, you should have several introductions that would allow you to move smoothly from the subject at hand into your testimony.

2. Memorize your major outline points and Scripture verses and practice until it becomes natural.

3. Smile! Ask God to give you a happy countenance. Use a natural speaking voice.

4. Be alert to nervous habits and avoid them. For example, jingling coins in your pocket, constantly clearing your throat, using "uh's" and "ah's", etc.

5. Don't argue! You can't drag a person into "the kingdom;" men are born of the Spirit, not by debate and persuasiveness.

NOTES

_____

_____

_____

_____

_____

_____

_____

NEXT ASSIGNMENT

Workbook Chapter:

Memory verse:

Meeting Location:

Date: Time:

Additional Notes:

_____

CHAPTER TWELVE

HOW TO HAVE A MINISTRY
Born to Reproduce*

Dawson E. Trotman

A few years ago, while visiting Edinburgh, Scotland, I stood on High Street just down from the castle. As I stood there, I saw a father and a mother coming toward me pushing a baby carriage. They looked very happy, were well dressed and apparently were well-to-do. I tried to catch a glimpse of the baby as they passed and, seeing my interest, they stopped to let me look at the litte, pink-cheeked member of their family.

I watched them for a little while as they walked on and thought how beautiful it is that God permits a man to choose one woman who seems the most beautiful and lovely to him, and she chooses him out of all the men whom she has ever known. Then they separate themselves to one another, and God in His plan gives them the means of reproduction! It is a wonderful thing that a little child should be born into their family, having some of the father's characteristics and some of the mother's, some of his looks and some of hers. Each sees in that baby a reflection of the one whom he or she loves.

Seeing that little one made me feel homesick for my own children whom I dearly love and whose faces I had not seen for some time. As I continued to stand there I saw another baby carriage, or perambulator as they call it over there, coming in my direction. It was a secondhand affair and very wobbly. Obviously the father and mother were poor. Both were dressed poorly and plainly, but when I indicated my interest in seeing their baby, they stopped and with the same pride as the other parents let me view their little, pink-cheeked, beautiful-eyed child.

I thought as these went on their way, "God give this little baby whose parents are poor everything that He gave the other. It has five little fingers on each hand, a little mouth and two eyes. Properly cared for, those little hands may someday be the hands of an artist or a musician."

* c 1975 by The Navigators
Used by permission

All rights reserved, including translation
All verses in this article are from King James Version.

Then this other thought came to me, "Isn't it wonderful that God did not select the wealthy and the educated to say, 'You can have children,' and to the poor and the uneducated say, 'You cannot.' Everyone on earth has that privilege."

The first order ever given to man was that he "be fruitful and multiply." In other words, he was to reproduce after his own kind. God did not tell Adam and Eve, our first parents, to be spiritual. They were already in His image. Sin had not yet come in. He just said, "Multiply. I want more just like you, more in My own image."

Of course, the image was marred. But Adam and Eve had children. They began to multiply. There came a time, however, when God had to destroy most of the flesh that had been born. He started over with eight people. The more than two billion people who are on the earth today came from the eight who were in the ark because they were fruitful and multiplied.

Hindrances

Only a few things will ever keep human beings from multiplying themselves in the physical realm. One is that they never marry. If they are not united, they will not reproduce. This is a truth which Christians need to grasp with reference to spiritual reproduction. When a person becomes a child of God, he should realize that he is to live in union with Jesus Christ if he is going to win others to the Saviour.

Another factor that can hinder reproduction is disease or impairment to some part of the body that is needed for reproductive purposes. In the spiritual realm sin is the disease that can keep one from winning the lost.

One other thing that can keep people from having children is immaturity. God in His wisdom saw to it that little children cannot have babies. A little boy must first grow to sufficient maturity to be able to earn a living, and a little girl must be old enough to care for a baby.

Everyone should be born again. That is God's desire. God never intended that man should merely live and die—be a walking corpse to be laid in the ground. The vast majority of people know that there is something beyond the grave, and so each one who is born into God's family should seek others to be born again.

A person is born again when he receives Jesus Christ. "But as many as received Him, to them gave He power to become the sons of God . . . Which were born, not of blood, nor of the will of the flesh, nor of the will of man, but of God" (John 1:12,13)—the new birth. It is God's plan that these new babes in Christ grow. All provision is made for their growth into maturity, and then they are to multiply—not only the rich or the educated, but all alike. Every person who is born into God's family is to multiply.

In the physical realm when your children have children, you become a grandparent. Your parents are then great-grandparents, and theirs are great-great-grandparents. And so it should be in the spiritual.

Spiritual Babes

Wherever you find a Christian who is not leading men and women to Christ, something is wrong. He may still be a babe. I do not mean that he does not know a lot of doctrine and is not well informed through hearing good preaching. I know many people who can argue the pre-, the post- and the amillennial position and who know much about dispensations, but who are still immature. Paul said of some such in Corinth, "And I, brethren, could not speak unto you as unto spiritual (or mature), but as unto carnal, even as unto babes . . ." (1 Corinthians 3:1).

Because they were babes, they were immature, incapable of spiritual reproduction. In other words, they could not help other people to be born again. Paul continued, "I have fed you with milk, and not with meat: for hitherto ye were not able to bear it . . . ye are yet carnal (or babes): for . . . there is among you envying, and strife, and divisions . . ." (1 Corinthians 3:2,3). I know a lot of church members, Sunday school teachers and members of the women's missionary society who will say to each other, "Have you heard about so and so?" and pass along some gossip. Such have done an abominable thing in the sight of God. How horrible it is when a Christian hears something and spreads the story! The Book says, "These six things doth the Lord hate: yea, seven are an abomination unto Him . . . a lying tongue . . ." (Proverbs 6:16,17). Oh, the Christians I know, both men and women, who let lying come in!

". . . he that soweth discord among brethren" (Proverbs 6:19) is another. This is walking as a babe, and I believe that it is one of the basic reasons why some Christians do not have people born again into God's family through them. They are sick spiritually. There is something wrong. There is a spiritual disease in their lives. They are immature. There is not that union with Christ.

But when all things are right between you and the Lord, regardless of how much or how little you may know intellectually from the standpoint of the world, you can be a spiritual parent. And that, incidentally, may even be when you are very young in the Lord.

A young lady works at the telephone desk in our office in Colorado Springs. A year and a half ago she was associated with the young Communist league in Great Britain. She heard Billy Graham and accepted the Lord Jesus Christ. Soon she and a couple other girls in her art and drama school were used of the Lord to win some girls to Christ. We taught Pat and some of the others, and they in turn taught the girls whom they led to Christ. Some of these have led still other girls to Christ, and they too are training their friends. Patricia is a great-grandmother already, though she is only about a year and four months old in the Lord.

We see this all the time. I know a sailor who, when he was only four months old in the Lord, was a great-grandfather. He had led some sailors to the Lord who in turn led other sailors to the Lord, and these last led still other sailors to the Lord—yet he was only four months old.

How was this done? God used the pure channel of these young Christians' lives in their exuberance and first love for Christ, and out of their hearts the incorruptible seed of the Word of God was sown in the hearts of other people. It took hold. Faith came by the hearing of the Word. They were born again by faith in the Lord Jesus Christ. They observed those Christians who led them to Christ and shared in the joy, the peace and the thrill of it all. And in their joy, they wanted someone else to know.

In every Christian audience, I am sure there are men and women who have been Christians for five, ten or twenty years but who do not know of one person who is living for Jesus Christ today because of them. I am not talking now about merely working for Christ, but about producing for Christ. Someone may say, "I gave out a hundred thousand tracts." That is good, but how many sheep did you bring in?

Some time ago I talked to 29 missionary candidates. They were graduates of universities or Bible schools or seminaries. As a member of the board I interviewed each one over a period of five days, giving each candidate from half an hour to an hour. Among the questions I asked were two which are very important. The first one had to do with their devotional life. "How is your devotional life?" I asked them. "How is the time you spend with the Lord? Do you feel that your devotional life is what the Lord would have it to be?"

Out of this particular group of 29 only one person said, "I believe my devotional life is what it ought to be." To the others my question then was, "Why is your devotional life not what it should be?"

"Well, you see, I am here at this summer institute," was a common reply. "We have a concentrated course. We do a year's work in only ten weeks. We are so busy."

I said, "All right. Let's back up to when you were in college. Did you have victory in your devotional life then?"

"Well, not exactly."

We traced back and found that never since they came to know the Saviour had they had a period of victory in their devotional lives. That was one of the reasons for their sterility—lack of communion with Christ.

The other question I asked them was. "You are going out to the foreign field. You hope to be used by the Lord in winning men and women to Christ. Is that right?"

"Yes."

"You want them to go on and live the victorious life, don't you? You don't want them just to make a decision and then go back into the world, do you?"

"No."

"Then may I ask you something more? How many persons do you know by name today who were won to Christ by you and are living for Him?"

The majority had to admit that they were ready to cross an ocean and learn a foreign language, but they had not won their first soul who was going on with Jesus Christ. A number of them said that they got many people to go to church; others said they had persuaded some to go forward when the invitation was given.

I asked,"Are they living for Christ now?" Their eyes dropped. I then continued, "How do you expect that by crossing an ocean and speaking in a foreign language with people who are suspicious of you, whose way of life is unfamiliar, you will be able to do there what you have not yet done here?"

These questions do not apply to missionaries and prospective missionaries only. They apply to all of God's people. Every one of His children ought to be a reproducer.

Are you producing? If not, why not? Is it because of a lack of communion with Christ, your Lord, that closeness of fellowship which is part of the great plan? Or is it some sin in your life, an unconfessed something, that has stopped the flow? Or is it that you are still a babe? "For when for the time ye ought to be teachers, ye have need that one teach you again . . ." (Hebrews 5:12).

How to Produce Reproducers

The reason that we are not getting this Gospel to the ends of the earth is not because it is not potent enough.

Twenty-three years ago we took a born-again sailor and spent some time with him, showing him how to reproduce spiritually after his kind. It took time, lots of time. It was not a hurried, 30-minute challenge in a church service and a hasty good-bye with an invitation to come back next week. We spent time together. We took care of his problems and taught him not only to hear God's Word and to read it, but also how to study it. We taught him how to fill the quiver of his heart with the arrows of God's Word, so that the Spirit of God could lift an arrow from his heart and place it to the bow of his lips and pierce a heart for Christ.

He found a number of boys on his ship, but none of them would go all out for the Lord. They would go to church, but when it came right down to doing something, they were "also rans." He came to me after a month of this and said,

"Dawson, I can't get any of these guys on the ship to get down to business."

I said to him, "Listen, you ask God to give you one. You can't have two until you have one. Ask God to give you a man after your own heart."

He began to pray. One day he came to me and said, "I think I've found him." Later he brought the young fellow over. Three months from the time that I started to work with him, he had found a man of like heart. This first sailor was not the kind of man you had to push and give prizes to before he would do something. He loved the Lord and was willing to pay a price to produce. He worked with this new babe in Christ, and those two fellows began to grow and spiritually reproduce. On that ship 125 men found the Saviour before it was sunk at Pearl Harbor. Men off that first battleship are in four continents of the world as missionaries today. It was necessary to make a start, however. The devil's great trick is to stop anything like this if he can before it gets started. He will stop you, too, if you let him.

There are Christians whose lives run in circles who, nevertheless, have the desire to be spiritual parents. Take a typical example. You meet him in the morning as he goes to work and say to him, "Why are you going to work?"

"Well, I have to earn money."

"What are you earning money for?" you ask.

"Well," he replies, "I have to buy food."

"What do you want food for?"

"I have to eat so as to have strength to go to work and earn some more money."

"What do you want more money for?"

"I have to buy clothes so that I can be dressed to go to work and earn some more money."

"What do you want more money for?"

"I have to buy a house or pay the rent so I will have a place to rest up, so I will be fit to work and earn some more money." And so it goes. There are many Christians like that who are going in big circles. But you continue your questioning and ask, "What else do you do?"

"Oh, I find time to serve the Lord. I am preaching here and there." But down behind all of this he has the one desire to be a spiritual father. He is praying that God will give him a man to teach. It may take six months. It need not take that long, but maybe it takes him six months to get him started taking in the Word and giving it out and getting ready to teach a man himself.

So this first man at the end of six months has another man. Each man starts teaching another in the following six months. At the end of the year, there are just four of them. Perhaps each one teaches a Bible class or helps in a street meeting, but at the same time his main interest is in his man and how he is doing. So at the end of the year the four of them get together and have a prayer meeting and determine, "Now, let's not allow anything to sidetrack us. Let's give the Gospel out to a lot of people, but let's check up on at least one man and see him through."

So the four of them in the next six months each get a man. That makes eight at the end of a year and a half. They all go out after another and at the end of two years there are 16 men. At the end of three years there are 64; the 16 have doubled twice. At the end of five years there are 1,048. At the end of fifteen and a half years there are 2,176,000,000. That is the present population of the world of persons over three years of age.

But wait a minute! Suppose that after the first man, A, helps B and B is ready to get his man while A starts helping another, B gets sidetracked, washes out and does not produce his first man. Fifteen and one-half years later you can cut your 2,176,000,000 down to 1,088,000,000 because the devil caused B to be sterile.

God promised Abraham ". . . in Isaac shall thy seed be called" (Genesis 21:12), so Abraham waited a long, long time for that son. God's promise to make Abraham the father of many nations was all wrapped up in that one son, Isaac. If Hitler had been present and had caused Isaac's death when Abraham had his knife poised over him on Mount Moriah, Hitler could have killed every Jew in that one stroke.

I believe that is why Satan puts all his efforts into getting the Christian busy, busy, busy, but not producing.

Men, where is your man? Women, where is your woman? Where is your girl? Where is the one whom you led to Christ and who is now going on with Him?

There is a story in 1 Kings, chapter 20 about a man who gave a prisoner to a servant and instructed the servant to guard the prisoner well. But as the servant was busy here and there the prisoner made his escape.

The curse of today is that we are too busy. I am not talking about being busy earning money to buy food. I am talking about being busy doing Christian things. We have spiritual activity with little productivity. And productivity comes as a result of what we call "follow-up."

Majoring In Reproducing

Five years ago Billy Graham came to me and said, "Daws, we would like you to help with our follow-up. I've been studying the great evangelists and the great revivals and I fail to see that there was much of a follow-up program. We need it. We are having an average of 6,000 people come forward to decide for Christ in a month's campaign. I feel that with the work you have done you could come in and help us."

I said, "Billy, I can't follow up 6,000 people. My work is always with individuals and small groups."

"Look, Daws," he answered, "everywhere I go I meet Navigators. I met them in school in Wheaton. They are in my school right now. (He was president of Northwestern Schools at that time.) There must be something to this."

"I just don't have the time," I said.

He tackled me again. The third time he pled with me and said, "Daws, I am not able to sleep nights for thinking of what happens to the converts after a crusade is over."

At that time I was on my way to Formosa and I said, "While I am there I will pray about it, Billy." On the sands of a Formosan beach I paced up and down two or three hours a day praying, "Lord, how can I do this? I am not even getting the work done You have given me to do. How can I take six months of the year to give to Billy?" But God laid the burden upon my heart.

Why should Billy have asked me to do it? I had said to him that day before I left for Formosa, "Billy, you will have to get somebody else."

He took me by the shoulders and said, "Who else? Who is majoring in this?" I had been majoring in it.

What will it take to jar us out of our complacency and send us home to pray, "God, give me a girl or man whom I can win to Christ, or let me take one who is already won, an infant in Christ, and try to train that one so that he or she will reproduce!"

How thrilled we are to see the masses fill up the seats! But where is your man? I would rather have one "Isaac" alive than a hundred dead, or sterile, or immature.

Beginning of Follow-up

One day years ago, I was driving along in my little Model T Ford and saw a young man walking down the street. I stopped and picked him up. As he got into the car, he swore and said, "It's sure tough to get a ride." I never hear a man take my Saviour's name in vain but what my heart aches. I reached into my pocket for a tract and said, "Lad, read this."

He looked up at me and said, "Haven't I seen you somewhere before?"

I looked at him closely. He looked like someone I should know. We figured out that we had met the year before on the same road. He was on his way to a golf course to caddy when I picked him up. He had gotten into my car and had started out the same way with the name "Jesus Christ." I had taken exception to his use of that name and had opened up the New Testament and shown him the way of salvation. He had accepted Jesus Christ as his Saviour. In parting I had given him Philippians 1:6, "Being confident of this very thing, that He which hath begun a good work in you will perform it until the day of Jesus Christ." "God bless you, son. Read this," I said, and sped on my merry way.

A year later, there was no more evidence of the new birth and the new creature in this boy than if he had never heard of Jesus Christ.

I had a great passion to win souls and that was my great passion. But after I met this boy the second time on the way to the golf course, I began to go back and find some of my "converts." I want to tell you, I was sick at heart. It seemed that Philippians 1:6 was not working.

An Armenian boy came into my office one day and told me about all the souls he had won. He said that they were all Armenians and had the list to prove it.

I said, "Well, what is this one doing?"

He said, "That one isn't doing so good. He is backslidden."

"What about this one?" We went all down the list and there was not one living a victorious life.

I said, "Give me your Bible." I turned to Philippians and put a cardboard right under the 6th verse, took a razor blade out of my pocket and started to come down on the page. He grabbed my hand and asked, "What are you going to do?"

"I'm going to cut this verse out," I said. "It isn't working."

Do you know what was wrong? I had been taking the 6th verse away from its context, verses 3 through 7. Paul was not just saying, "All right, the Lord has started something, He will finish it." But you know, that is what some people tell me when they win a soul. They say, "Well, I just committed him to God."

Suppose I meet someone who has a large family and say to him, "Who is taking care of your children?"

"My family? Oh, I left them with the Lord."

Right away I would say to that one, "I have a verse for you: 'But if any provide not for his own, and specially for those of his own house, he . . . is worse than an infidel' (1 Timothy 5:8)."

Paul said to the elders of the church at Ephesus, "Take heed . . . to all the flock, over the which the Holy Ghost hath made you overseers . . ." (Acts 20:28). You cannot make God the overseer. He makes you the overseer.

We began to work on follow-up. This emphasis on finding and helping some of the converts went on for a couple or three years before the Navigator work started. By that time our work included fewer converts but more time spent with the converts. Soon I could say as Paul said to the Philippians, "I thank my God upon every remembrance of you, Always in every prayer of mine for you all making request with joy, For your fellowship in the Gospel from the first day until now" (Philippians 1:3-5). He followed up his converts with daily prayer and fellowship. Then he could say, "Being confident of this very thing, that He which hath begun a good work in you will perform it until the day of Jesus Christ" (Philippians 1:6). In keeping with this the 7th verse reads: "Even as it is meet (or proper) for me to think this of you all, because I have you in my heart . . ."

Before I had forgotten to follow up the people God had reached through me. But from then on I began to spend time helping them. That is why sometime later when that first sailor came to me, I saw the value of spending three months with him. I saw an Isaac in him. Isaac had Jacob, and Jacob had the twelve, and all the rest of the nation came through them.

It Takes Time to Do God's Work

You can lead a soul to Christ in from 20 minutes to a couple of hours. But it takes from 20 weeks to a couple of years to get him on the road to maturity, victorious over the sins and the recurring problems that come along. He must learn how to make right decisions. He must be warned of the various "isms" that are likely to reach out with their octopus arms and pull him in and sidetrack him.

But when you get yourself a man, you have doubled your ministry—in fact, you have more than doubled your ministry. Do you know why? When you teach your man, he sees how it is done and he imitates you.

If I were the minister of a church and had deacons or elders to pass the plate and choir members to sing, I would say, "Thank God for your help. We need you. Praise the Lord for these extra things that you do," but I would keep pressing home the big job—"Be fruitful and multiply." All these other things are incidental to the supreme task of winning a man or woman to Jesus Christ and then helping him or her to go on.

Where is your man? Where is your woman? Do you have one? You can ask God for one. Search your hearts. Ask the Lord, "Am I spiritually sterile? If I am, why am I?"

Don't let your lack of knowledge stand in the way. It used to be the plan of The Navigators in the early days that whenever the sailors were with us for supper each fellow was asked at the end of the meal to quote a verse.

I would say it this way, "Quote a verse you have learned in the last 48 hours if you have one. Otherwise, just give us a verse." One evening as we quoted verses around the table, my little three-year-old daughter's turn came. There was a new sailor next to her who did not think about her quoting Scripture, so without giving her an opportunity, he began. She looked up at him as much as to say, "I am a human being," then she quoted John 3:16 in her own way. "For God so loved the world, dat He gave His only forgotten Son, dat *whosoever* believeth in Him should not perish, but have everlasting life." She put the emphasis on the "whosoever" because when she was first taught the verse she could not pronounce that word.

Days later that sailor came over and said to me, "You know, I was going to quote that verse of Scripture. It was the only one I knew. But I didn't really know it, not until little Ruthie quoted it. When she said 'whosoever,' I thought, 'that means me.' Back on the ship I accepted the Lord." Today that young man is a missionary in South America.

Until several years after we were married, my wife's father did not know the Lord. Here again God used children to reach a hungry heart. When Ruthie was three and Bruce was five, they went to visit Grandpa and Grandma. Grandpa tried to get them to repeat nursery rhymes. He said, "Mary had a little lamb" and "Little Boy Blue," but the children just looked at him and asked, "Who is Little Boy Blue?" He thought they did not know very much.

Their mother said, "They know some things. Quote Romans 3:23, Bruce." This Bruce did. Then he asked, "Shall I quote another one, Grandpa?"

"Sure," said Grandpa.

Bruce began to quote verses of Scripture, some 15 in all, and Ruth quoted some in between. This delighted Grandpa. He took them over to the neighbors and to the aunts and uncles, showing them how well these children knew the Scriptures. In the meantime the Word of God was doing its work. It was not long before the Holy Spirit, through the voices of babes, planted the seed in his heart. "Out of the mouth of babes and sucklings hast Thou ordained strength . . ." (Psalm 8:2).

Soulwinners are not soulwinners because of what they know, but because of the Person they know, how well they know Him and how much they long for others to know Him.

"Oh, but I am afraid," someone says. Remember, "The fear of man bringeth a snare: but whoso putteth his trust in the Lord shall be safe" (Proverbs 29:25). Nothing under heaven except sin, immaturity and lack of communion will put you in a position where you cannot reproduce. Furthermore, there is not anything under heaven that can keep a newly born again one from going on with the Lord if he has a spiritual parent to take care of him and give him the spiritual food God has provided for his normal growth.

Effects obey their causes by irresistible laws. When you sow the seed of God's Word you will get results. Not every heart will receive the Word but some will and the new birth will take place. When a soul is born, give it the care that Paul gave new believers. Paul believed in follow-up work. He was a busy evangelist, but he took time for follow-up. The New Testament is largely made up of the letters of Paul which were follow-up letters to the converts.

James believed in it. "But be ye doers of the Word, and not hearers only," he said in James 1:22. Peter believed in it. "As newborn babes, desire the sincere milk of the Word, that ye may grow thereby" (1 Peter 2:2). John believed in it, "I have no greater joy than to hear that my children walk in truth" (3 John 4). All the writings of Peter, Paul, James and most of John's are food for the new Christian.

The Gospel spread to the known world during the first century without radio, television or the printing press, because of men who were reproducing. But today we have a lot of pew-sitters—people think that if they are faithful in church attendance, put good-sized gifts into the offering plate and get people to come, they have done their part.

Where is your man? Where is your woman? Where is your boy? Where is your girl? Every one of us, no matter what age we are, should get busy memorizing Scripture. In one Sunday school class a woman 72 years of age and another who was 78 finished The Navigators Topical Memory System. They then had something to give.

Load your heart with this precious Seed. You will find that God will direct you to those whom you can lead to Christ. There are many hearts ready for the Gospel now.

BORN TO REPRODUCE

1. What does it mean to be a "spiritual parent?" _____

_____

2. What are some of the hindrances to spiritual reproduction?

a. _____

b. _____

c. _____

3. How old (in the Lord) do you have to be before you can reproduce spiritually?

_____

4 How much do you have to **know** before you can be a spiritual reproducer?

_____

5. What is the difference between "work" for Christ and "producing" for Christ?

_____

_____

> Dawson Trotman introduces the concept of spiritual multiplication. He notes that this is the key to spiritual productivity. Let's explore this important concept.

Praying and giving are two important ways of helping reach the world for Jesus Christ with his gospel. An even more direct way we can be involved is through our personal witness. Now is the time to begin reaching the world for Christ. We must not wait until we think we are fully trained, or even until we feel a personal call. As Christians we have already been called to this task!

6. For what ministry does the Holy Spirit empower us? *Acts 1:8*

_____

_____

_____

Of course the world will not be reached by the witness of a single individual. God wants us to reach the world in the same way it is populated—by multiplication. Man has carried out God's command to Noah in Genesis 9:1—to multiply physically. In the same way, it is possible to multiply spiritually.

7. Read Paul's instructions to Timothy in 2 Timothy 2:2.

a. What did Paul tell Timothy to do?

_____

_____

b. What kind of man did Paul tell Timothy to invest his life in?

_____

Communication passes from one person to another. In this verse, Paul's instruction was passed to Timothy, who was to pass it on to reliable men who would pass it on to others.

As you invest your life in one man and then see him invest his life in the life of another, you will become part of the spiritual multiplication process.

8. None of us knows how long we are going to live. But for the moment, suppose you will live until you are 70 years old. If this were so, how many years do you have left to invest your life in the lives of others? _____

*Adapted from Design for Discipleship
© 1973, 1978 by The Navigators
Used by permission

A Christian should be able to help a younger believer grow at such a pace that in two years the person being helped is ready to help another grow as well. Every two years you would help someone else reach this point. Do you think this is reasonable for your life?

If it is, then in two years you and another person can have started the multiplication process.

- In four years there would be four people.
- In six years there would be eight people.
- In eight years there would be sixteen people, and so on.

Considering how many years you anticipate you can minister, calculate how many people you can affect during the rest of your life.

HOW DO YOU FIT IN?

Jesus loved the world and helped thousands, *but he closely trained only twelve men.* The ministry of multiplying disciples comes through ministry to individuals. This is the way Paul communicated his life to Timothy (see 2 Timothy 3:10). We reach the masses through the man.

Ask God to give you one person with whom you can put 2 Timothy 2:2 into action. You can help change the world for Jesus Christ by allowing God to reproduce His life through you in the life of another.

Ask your leader to give you a copy of the Operation Timothy Leader's Guide and explain how you can find and recruit God's man for you. Then, get ready for the adventure of your life. You are about to embark on a challenge that excited men for nearly 2000 years — the opportunity to become directly and vitally involved in God's strategy to reach the world.

PRAYER REQUESTS

Date	Request	Update/Answer Date

The Word of God KJV

Timothy 3:16-17

All scripture is given by inspiration of God, and is profitable for doctrine, for reproof, for correction, for instruction in righteousness. That the man of God may be perfect, thoroughly furnished until all good works.

2 Timothy 3:16-17

Assurance of Guidance KJV

Proverbs 3:5-6

Trust in the Lord with all thine heart, and lean not unto thine own understanding. In all thy ways acknowledge him, and he shall direct thy paths.

Proverbs 3:5-6

Obedience to Christ KJV

Romans 12:1-2

I beseech you therefore, brethren, by the mercies of God, that ye present your bodies a living sacrifice, holy, acceptable unto God, which is your reasonable service. And be not conformed to this world, but be ye transformed by the renewing of your mind, that ye may prove what is that good, and acceptable, and perfect, will of God.

Romans 12:1-2

10 The Power to Witness KJV

Acts 1:8

But ye shall receive power, after that the Holy Ghost is come upon you, and ye shall be witnesses unto me both in Jerusalem, and in all Judea, and in Samaria, and unto the uttermost part of the earth.

Acts 1:8

11 The Call to Witness KJV

1 Peter 3:15

But sanctify the Lord God in your hearts, and be ready always to give an answer to every man that asketh you a reason of the hope that is in you with meekness and fear.

1 Peter 3:15

12 Discipleship KJV

2 Timothy 2:2

And the things that thou hast heard of me among many witnesses, the same commit thou to faithful men, who shall be able to teach others also.

2 Timothy 2:2

MOST 10 WANTED

1.
2.
3.
4.
5.
6.
7.
8.
9.
10.

I will faithfully pray for the salvation of the above and will attempt to reach them for Christ through personal witness and CBMC outreach efforts.

"The earnest prayer of a righteous man has great effect." James 5:16

10 The Power to Witness

NIV

Acts 1:8
But you will receive power when the Holy Spirit comes on you, and you will be my witnesses in Jerusalem, and in all Judea and Samaria, and to the ends of the earth.

Acts 1:8

11 The Call to Witness

NIV

1 Peter 3:15
But in your hearts set apart Christ as Lord. Always be prepared to give an answer to everyone who asks you to give the reason for the hope that you have.

1 Peter 3:15

12 Discipleship

NIV

2 Timothy 2:2
And the things you have heard me say in the presence of many witnesses entrust to reliable men who will also be qualified to teach others.

2 Timothy 2:2

7 The Word of God

N

2 Timothy 3:16-17
All Scripture is God-breathed and is useful teaching, rebuking, correcting and training righteousness, so that the man of God may thoroughly equipped for every good work.

2 Timothy 3:16-

8 Assurance of Guidance

N

Proverbs 3:5-6
Trust in the Lord with all your heart and lean no on your own understanding, in all your way acknowledge him, and he will make your path straight.

Proverbs 3:5-

9 Obedience to Christ

N

Romans 12:1-2
Therefore, I urge you, brothers, in view of God mercy, to offer your bodies as living sacrifices, ho and pleasing to God—which is your spiritual worship Do not conform any longer to the pattern of th world, but be transformed by the renewing of you mind. Then you will be able to test and approve wha God's will is—his good, pleasing and perfect will.

Romans 12:1-

MOST **10** WANTED

1.
2.
3.
4.
5.
6.
7.
8.
9.
10.

I will faithfully pray for the salvation of the above and will attempt to reach them for Christ through personal witness and CBMC outreach efforts.

"The earnest prayer of a righteous man has great effect." James 5:16

Made in United States
Troutdale, OR
09/07/2023

12727264R00040